THE LOST

OTHER BOOKS BY EAVAN BOLAND

POETRY

New Territory

The War Horse

Night Feed

The Journey

Selected Poems: 1989

Outside History: Selected Poems 1980–1990

In a Time of Violence

An Origin Like Water: Collected Poems 1967–1987

PROSE

Object Lessons:
The Life of the Woman and the Poet in Our Time

THE
LOST LAND

P O E M S

EAVAN BOLAND

W · W · NORTON & COMPANY

NEW YORK   LONDON

Printed in the United States of America

First published as a Norton paperback 1999

For information about permission to reproduce selections from this book,
write to Permissions, W. W. Norton & Company, Inc., 500 Fifth Avenue,
New York, NY 10110.

The text of this book is composed in 12.5/16 Centaur MT
with the display set in Felix Titling.
Composition by JoAnn Schambier.
Manufacturing by Courier Companies, Inc.
Book design by Margaret M. Wagner.

Library of Congress Cataloging-in-Publication Data
Boland, Eavan.
The lost land / Eavan Boland.
p.   cm.
ISBN 0-393-04663-X
1. Women—Ireland—Poetry. 1. Title.
PR6052.035L67   1998
821'.914—dc21   98-3214
                                          CIP
ISBN 0-393-31951-2 pbk
ISBN 978-0-393-31951-4

W. W. Norton & Company, Inc., 500 Fifth Avenue, New York, N.Y. 10110
http://www.wwnorton.com

W. W. Norton & Company Ltd., Castle House, 75/76 Wells Street, London W1T 3QT

3 4 5 6 7 8 9 0

FOR
MARY ROBINSON—
WHO FOUND IT

CONTENTS

ACKNOWLEDGMENTS

Selections from this book have appeared in the following:

P.N.Review
Princeton Library Chronicle
The New Yorker
American Poetry Review
Poetry
Notre Dame Review
Waterstone's Chronicle
The Irish Times

"The Harbour" was published in *Ecstatic Occasions, Expedient Forms,*
edited by David Lehman and published by the University of
Michigan Press.

I would like to thank Jill Bialosky, Jody Allen-Randolph, and
Kevin Casey for their readings.

COLONY

I. My Country in Darkness

After the wolves and before the elms
the bardic order ended in Ireland.

Only a few remained to continue
a dead art in a dying land:

This is a man
on the road from Youghal to Cahirmoyle.
He has no comfort, no food and no future.
He has no fire to recite his friendless measures by.
His riddles and flatteries will have no reward.
His patrons sheath their swords in Flanders and Madrid.

Reader of poems, lover of poetry—
in case you thought this was a gentle art
follow this man on a moonless night
to the wretched bed he will have to make:

The Gaelic world stretches out under a hawthorn tree
and burns in the rain. This is its home,
its last frail shelter. All of it—
Limerick, the Wild Geese and what went before—
falters into cadence before he sleeps:
He shuts his eyes. Darkness falls on it.

2. The Harbour

This harbour was made by art and force.
And called Kingstown and afterwards Dun Laoghaire.
And holds the sea behind its barrier
less than five miles from my house.

Lord be with us say the makers of a nation.
Lord look down say the builders of a harbour.
They came and cut a shape out of ocean
and left stone to close around their labour.

Officers and their wives promenaded
on this spot once and saw with their own eyes
the opulent horizon and obedient skies
which nine tenths of the law provided.

And frigates with thirty-six guns, cruising
the outer edges of influence, could idle
and enter here and catch the tide of
empire and arrogance and the Irish Sea rising

and rising through a century of storms
and cormorants and moonlight the whole length of this coast,
while an ocean forgot an empire and the armed
ships under it changed: to slime weed and cold salt and rust.

«

City of shadows and of the gradual
capitulations to the last invader
this is the final one: signed in water
and witnessed in granite and ugly bronze and gun-metal.

And by me. I am your citizen: composed of
your fictions, your compromise, I am
a part of your story and its outcome.
And ready to record its contradictions.

3. Witness

Here is the city—
its worn-down mountains,
its grass and iron,
its smoky coast
seen from the high roads
on the Wicklow side.

From Dalkey Island
to the North Wall,
to the blue distance seizing its perimeter,
its old divisions are deep within it.

And in me also.
And always will be.

Out of my mouth they come:
The spurred and booted garrisons.
The men and women
they dispossessed.

What is a colony
if not the brutal truth
that when we speak
the graves open.

And the dead walk?

4. Daughters of Colony

Daughters of parsons and of army men.
Daughters of younger sons of younger sons.
Who left for London from Kingstown harbour—
never certain which they belonged to.

Who took their journals and their steamer trunks.
Who took their sketching books.

Who wore hats
made out of local straw
dried in an Irish field beside a river which

flowed to a town they had known in childhood,
and watched forever from their bedroom windows,
framed in the clouds and cloud-shadows,
the blotchy cattle and

the scattered window lamps of a flat landscape
they could not enter.
Would never enter.

I see the darkness coming.
The absurd smallness of the handkerchiefs
they are waving
as the shore recedes.

I put my words between them
and the silence
the failing light has consigned them to:

I also am a daughter of the colony.
I share their broken speech, their other-whereness.

No testament or craft of mine can hide
our presence
on the distaff side of history.

See: they pull the brims of their hats
down against a gust from the harbour.

They cover
their faces with what should have been
and never quite was: their home.

5. Imago

Head of a woman. Half-life of a nation.
Coarsely-cut blackthorn walking stick.
Old Tara brooch.
And bog oak.
A harp and a wolfhound on an ashtray.

All my childhood
I took you for the truth.

I see you now for what you are.

My ruthless images. My simulacra.
Anti-art: a foul skill
traded by history
to show a colony

the way to make pain a souvenir.

6. The Scar

Dawn on the river:
Dublin rises out of what reflects it:

Anna Liffey
looks to the east, to the sea,
her profile carved out by the light
on the old Carlisle bridge.

I was five
when a piece of glass
cut my head and left a scar.
Afterwards my skin felt different.

And still does on these autumn days when
the mist hides the city
from the Liffey.

The Liffey hides
the long ships, the muskets and the burning domes.

Everything but this momentary place.
And those versions of the Irish rain
which change the features
of a granite face.

(

If colony is a wound what will heal it?
After such injuries
what difference do we feel?

No answer in the air,
on the water, in the distance.
And yet

emblem of this old,
torn and traded city,
altered by its river, its weather,
I turn to you as if there were—

one flawed head towards another.

7. City of Shadows

When I saw my father
buttoning his coat at Front Gate
I thought he would look like a man
who had lost what he had. And he did:

Grafton Street and Nassau Street were gone.
And the old parliament at College Green.
And the bronze arms and attitudes of orators
from Grattan to O'Connell. All gone.

We went to his car. He got in.
I waved my hands and motioned him to turn
his wheel towards the road to the only
straight route out to the coast.

When he did
I walked beside the car,
beside the kerb, and we made our way
in dark inches to the Irish Sea.

Then I smelled salt
and heard the foghorn.
And realized suddenly that I
had brought my father to his destination.

         «

I walked home
alone to my flat.
The fog was lifting slowly. I thought
whatever the dawn made clear

and cast-iron and adamant again,
I would know from now on that in
a lost land of orators and pedestals,
and corners and street names and rivers,

where even the ground underfoot
was hidden from view, there had been
one way out.
And I found it.

8. Unheroic

It was an Irish summer it was wet.
It was a job. I was seventeen.
I set the clock and caught the bus at eight
and leaned my head against the misty window.
The city passed by. I got off
above the Liffey on a street of statues:
iron orators and granite patriots.
Arms wide. Lips apart. Last words.

I worked in a hotel. I carried trays.
I carried keys. I saw the rooms
when they were used and airless and again
when they were aired and ready and I stood
above the road and stared down at
silent eloquence and wet umbrellas.

There was a man who lived in the hotel.
He was a manager. I rarely saw him.
There was a rumour that he had a wound
from war or illness—no one seemed sure—
which would not heal. And when he finished
his day of ledgers and telephones he went
up the back stairs to his room
to dress it. I never found out
where it was. Someone said in his thigh.
Someone else said deep in his side.

He was a quiet man. He spoke softly.
I saw him once or twice on the stairs
at the back of the building by the laundry.
Once I waited, curious to see him.

Mostly I went home. I got my coat
and walked bare-headed to the river
past the wet, bronze and unbroken skin
of those who learned their time and knew their country.
How do I know my country? Let me tell you
it has been hard to do. And when I do
go back to difficult knowledge it is not
to that street or those men raised
high above the certainties they stood on—
Ireland hero history—but how

I went behind the linen room and up
the stone stairs and climbed to the top.
And stood for a moment there, concealed
by shadows. In a hiding place.
Waiting to see.
Wanting to look again.
Into the patient face of the unhealed.

9. The Colonists

I am ready to go home
through an autumn evening.

Suddenly,
without any warning, I can see them.

They form slowly out of the twilight.
Their faces. Arms. Greatcoats. And tears.

They are holding maps.
But the pages are made of fading daylight.
Their tears, made of dusk, fall across the names.

Although they know by heart
every inch and twist of the river
which runs through this town, and their houses—
every aspect of the light their windows found—
they cannot find where they come from:

The river is still there.
But not their town.
The light is there. But not their moment in it.

Then they faded.
And the truth is I never saw them.
If I had I would have driven home

through an ordinary evening, knowing
that not one street name or sign or neighbourhood

could be trusted
to the safe-keeping
of the making and unmaking of a people.

And have entered a house I might never
find again, and have written down—
as I do now—

their human pain. Their ghostly weeping.

10. A Dream of Colony

I dreamed we came to an iron gate.
And leaned against it.

It opened.
We heard it grinding slowly over gravel.

We began to walk.
When we started talking
I saw our words had the rare power
to unmake history:

Gradually the elms beside us
shook themselves into leaves.
And laid out under us their undiseased shadows.

Each phrase of ours,
holding still for a moment in the stormy air,
raised an unburned house
at the end of an avenue of elder and willow.

Unturned that corner
the assassin eased around and aimed from.
Undid. Unsaid:
Once. Fire. Quick. Over there.

        (

The scarred granite healed in my sleep.
The thundery air became sweet again.
We had come to the top of the avenue.

I heard laughter and forgotten consonants.
I saw greatcoats and epaulettes.
I turned to you—

but who are you?

Before I woke I heard a woman's voice cry out.
It was hoarse with doubt.
She was saying,
I was saying—

What have we done?

II. A Habitable Grief

Long ago
I was a child in a strange country:

I was Irish in England.

I learned
a second language there
which has stood me in good stead:

the lingua franca of a lost land.

A dialect in which
what had never been could still be found:

that infinite horizon. Always far
and impossible. That contrary passion
to be whole.

This is what language is:
a habitable grief. A turn of speech
for the everyday and ordinary abrasion
of losses such as this:

which hurts
just enough to be scar.

And heals just enough to be a nation.

12. The Mother Tongue

The old pale ditch can still be seen
less than half a mile from my house—

its ancient barrier of mud and brambles
which mireth next unto Irishmen
is now a mere rise of coarse grass,
a rowan tree and some thinned-out spruce,
where a child is playing at twilight.

I stand in the shadows. I find it
hard to believe now that once
this was a source of our division:

Dug. Drained. Shored up and left
to keep out and keep in. That here
the essence of a colony's defence
was the substance of the quarrel with its purpose:

Land. Ground. A line drawn in rain
and clay and the roots of wild broom—
behind it the makings of a city,
beyond it rumours of a nation—
by Dalkey and Kilternan and Balally
through two ways of saying their names.

A window is suddenly yellow.
A woman is calling a child.
She turns from her play and runs to her name.

Who came here under cover of darkness
from Glenmalure and the Wicklow hills
to the limits of this boundary? Who whispered
the old names for love to this earth
and anger and ownership as it opened
the abyss of their future at their feet?

I was born on this side of the Pale.
I speak with the forked tongue of colony.
But I stand in the first dark and frost
of a winter night in Dublin and imagine

my pure sound, my undivided speech
travelling to the edge of this silence.
As if to find me. And I listen: I hear
what I am safe from. What I have lost.

THE
LOST LAND

Home

Off a side road in southern California
is a grove of eucalyptus.
It looks as if
someone once came here with a handful

of shadows not seeds and planted them.
And they turned into trees.
But the leaves
have a tell-tale blueness and deepness.

Up a slope to the left is a creek.
Across it lies a cut-down tree trunk.
Further back again is the faraway,
filtered-out glitter of the Pacific.

I went there one morning with a friend
in mid-October
when the monarch butterflies
arrive from their westward migration:

thousands of them. Hundreds of thousands
collecting in a single location.

I climbed to the creek and looked up.
Every leaf was covered and ended in
a fluttering struggle.

Atmosphere. Ocean. Oxygen and dust
were altered by their purposes:
They had changed the trees to iron.
They were rust.

I looked at my watch. It was early.
But my mind was ready
for the evening
they were darkening into overhead:

Every inch and atom of daylight
was filled with their beating and flitting,
their rising and flying at the hour
when dusk falls on a coastal city

where I had my hands full of shadows.
Once. And planted them.
And they became
a suburb and a house and a doorway
entered by and open to an evening
every room was lighted to offset.

I once thought that a single word
had the power to change.
To transform.

"

But these had not been changed.
And I would not be changed by it again.

If I could not say the word *home*.
If I could not breathe the Irish night
air and inference of rain coming from the east,

I could at least be sure—
far below them and unmoved by movement—
of one house with its window, making

an oblong of wheat out of light.

The Lost Land

I have two daughters.

They are all I ever wanted from the earth.

Or almost all.

I also wanted one piece of ground:

One city trapped by hills. One urban river.
An island in its element.

So I could say *mine. My own.*
And mean it.

Now they are grown up and far away

and memory itself
has become an emigrant,
wandering in a place
where love dissembles itself as landscape:

Where the hills
are the colours of a child's eyes,
where my children are distances, horizons:

At night,
on the edge of sleep,

I can see the shore of Dublin Bay.
Its rocky sweep and its granite pier.

Is this, I say
how they must have seen it,
backing out on the mailboat at twilight,

shadows falling
on everything they had to leave?
And would love forever?
And then

I imagine myself
at the landward rail of that boat
searching for the last sight of a hand.

I see myself
on the underworld side of that water,
the darkness coming in fast, saying
all the names I know for a lost land:

Ireland. Absence. Daughter.

Mother Ireland

At first
   I was land
      I lay on my back to be fields
and when I turned
      on my side
            I was a hill
under freezing stars.
      I did not see.
          I was seen.
Night and day
      words fell on me.
          Seeds. Raindrops.
Chips of frost.
   From one of them
      I learned my name.
          I rose up. I remembered it.
Now I could tell my story.
   It was different
      from the story told about me.
And now also
   it was spring.
      I could see the wound I had left
in the land by leaving it.
      I travelled west.
          Once there
   I looked with so much love
      at every field

as it unfolded
        its rusted wheel and its pram chassis
                and at the gorse-
bright distances
   I had been
        that they misundersrtood me.
   Come back to us
they said.
        Trust me I whispered.

The Blossom

A May morning.
Light starting in the sky.

I have come here
after a long night.
Its senses of loss.
Its unrelenting memories of happiness.

The blossom on the apple tree is still in shadow,
its petals half-white and filled with water at the core,
in which the freshness and secrecy of dawn are stored
even in the dark.

How much longer
will I see girlhood in my daughter?

In other seasons
I knew every leaf on this tree.
Now I stand here
almost without seeing them

and so lost in grief
I hardly notice what is happening
as the light increases and the blossom speaks,
and turns to me
with blonde hair and my eyebrows and says—

"imagine if I stayed here,
even for the sake of your love,
what would happen to the summer?
To the fruit?

Then holds out a dawn-soaked hand to me,
whose fingers I counted at birth
years ago.

And touches mine for the last time.

And falls to earth.

Daughter

I. THE SEASON

The edge of spring.
The dark is wet. Already
stars are tugging at
their fibrous roots:

In February
they will fall and shine
from the roadsides
in their yellow hundreds.

My first child
was conceived in this season.
If I wanted a child now
I could not have one.

Except through memory.
Which is the ghost of the body.
Or myth.
Which is the ghost of meaning.

II. THE LOSS

All morning
the sound of chain saws.
My poplar tree has been cut down.

In dark spring dawns
when I could hardly raise
my head from the pillow

its sap rose
thirty feet into the air.
Into daylight. Into the last of starlight.

I go out to the garden
to touch the hurt wood spirits.
The injured summers.

Out of one of them a child runs.
Her skin printed with leaf-shadow.

And will not look at me.

III. THE BARGAIN

The garden creaks with rain.
The gutters run with noisy water.
The earth shows its age and makes a promise
only myth can keep. *Summer. Daughter.*

Ceres Looks at the Morning

I wake slowly. Already
my body is a twilight: Solid. Cold.
At the edge of a larger darkness. But outside
my window
a summer day is beginning. Apple trees
appear, one by one. Light is pouring
into the promise of fruit.

                       Beautiful morning
look at me as a daughter would
look: with that love and that curiosity:
as to what she came from.
And what she will become.

Tree of Life

A tree on a moonless night
has no sap or colour.

It has no flower and no fruit.

It waits for the sun to find them.

I cannot find you
in this dark hour
dear child.

Wait
for dawn to make us clear to one another.

Let the sun
inch above the roof-tops,

Let love
be the light that shows again

the blossom to the root.

*(Commissioned by the National Maternity Hospital, Dublin,
during its 1994 centenary, to mark a service to commemorate
the babies who had died there.)*

Escape

I

It was only when a swan
made her nest
on the verge beside Leeson Street bridge,

and too near the kerb by the canal,
that I remembered
my first attempt at an Irish legend.

And stopped the car
and walked over to her.
And into my twentieth winter:

I I

The window open where I left it.
The tablecloth still on the table.
The page at the last line I crafted.

I I I

I sat in the kitchen and frost
blended with kettle steam while
I crossed out and crossed out
the warm skin and huggable limbs
of Lir's children—

«

rhyming them into doomed swans
cursed into flight on
a coast that was only half a mile
from my flat in Morehampton Road.

   I V
It was evening now. Overhead
wild stars had wheels and landing gear.

A small air of spring hung above
the verge with its bottle lids and papers,
its poplar shadows,
its opening narcissi
and passers-by hurrying home from offices,
who barely turned to see what was there:

   V
A mother bird too near the road.

A middle-aged woman going
as near to her as she dared.

Neither of them willing
to stir from the actual and ordinary,
momentary danger.

One of them aware of the story.

Both of them escaped from the telling.

Dublin, 1959

The café had
plastic chairs and lunch counters.
Its doors opened out on O'Connell Street.

I hunched my knees
under the table. The vinegar bottle
shifted its bitter yellows.

Tell me a story about Ireland
I said as a child
to anyone in earshot: about what had been
left behind by a modern world.
But not by memory.

I remember
we paid for our tea with a single pound note.
And walked out. And a bicycle went by,
its bell ringing loudly. And a car swerved around it.

Watching Old Movies When
They Were New

I grew up in grey and white.
In half-tones and undertones.
Sitting by a bakelite telephone,
watching grainy and snowy kisses on the small screen.
This was New York.
I was thirteen. Outside my window the gardenless
and flowerless city, with its sirens
its cents, was new to me. And I was tired
of being anywhere but home. So I settled back
to grow older quickly.
And the crescent moon,
and the shirt-collar of that man
as he kissed the girl under it and her face
as she turned away and the ocean beginning
to burn and glisten in the distance:
they were like me: what they lacked was
outside them. Was an absence within which
they could only be
less than themselves: anyone could see
their doom was not love, was not destiny, was only
monochrome. But a time was coming. Is coming. Has come
and gone. And I will know what I am watching is
a passionate economy
we call the past. Although
its other name may be memory. And somewhere else
the future is already growing consequences. They are blue
and yellow. They are vermilion or a vivid green.

Pick us, they will say. *Bring us indoors.*
Arrange us into a city.
Into a situation. See how quickly
you tire of us. How soon you will yearn
for these tones and coolnesses. I know
nothing of this as I lean back. As the screen flickers.

Happiness

A Connemara summer. 1940.
My father is learning Irish.
My mother
is painting the harvest.

She holds umber and burnt orange
up against the canvas.

He says
samradh for summer and *atais* for happiness.

The Atlantic
salts the dark. She packs her colours.

It is time to go home
to the city where I have yet to be born:

They cannot see my sadness as the train
moves east through fields, shadows, farms
towards my life.

They do not hear the wheels
saying—as I can—

never again, never again.

Heroic

Sex and history. And skin and bone.
And the oppression of Sunday afternoon.
Bells called the faithful to devotion.

I was still at school and on my own.
And walked and walked and sheltered from the rain.

The patriot was made of drenched stone.
His lips were still speaking. The gun
he held had just killed someone.

I looked up. And looked at him again.
He stared past me without recognition.

I moved my lips and wondered how the rain
would taste if my tongue were made of stone.
And wished it was. And whispered so that no one
could hear it but him: *make me a heroine.*

The Last Discipline

In the evening
after a whole day at the easel
my mother would put down her brush,
pour turpentine into a glass jar,
and walk to the table.

Then she took a mirror,
hand-sized, enamelled in green,
and turned her back to the canvas.
And stood there.
And looked in it.

It was dusk.
The sheets were ghostly.
The canvas was almost not there.
In the end all I could see was her hand
closed around the handle.

All I can see now
is her hand, her head.
Her back is turned to what she made.
The mirror shows her
what is over her shoulder:

a room in winter.
A window with fog outside it.
A painting she sees is not finished.
A child. Her face round with impatience,
who will return,

who has returned,
who only knows now that she has seen
the rare and necessary—
usually unobservable—
last discipline.

The Proof That Plato
Was Wrong

August. And already
     light is assembling   .
another season at
     the end of an avenue
of water every tree is
     getting ready to
shed its leaves under.
     I was young here.
I am older here.
     I have come here
to find courage in
     the way this dawn
reaches slowly down
     the canal and reveals
a drowned summer
     which is almost over.
In the submarine
     greenness of these trees
whose roots and sinews
     are only—after all—
rain. And in these birds
     which cannot be heard,
which will never be
     heard. But are still

beginning to
        raise their heads
and open out
        their flooded wings,
as if they had not
        forgotten what
song is.

The Necessity for Irony

On Sundays,
when the rain held off,
after lunch or later,
I would go with my twelve year old
daughter into town,
and put down the time
at junk sales, antique fairs.

There I would
lean over tables,
absorbed by
lace, wooden frames,
glass. My daughter stood
at the other end of the room,
her flame-coloured hair
obvious whenever—
which was not often—

I turned around.
I turned around.
She was gone.
Grown. No longer ready
to come with me, whenever
a dry Sunday
held out its promises
of small histories. Endings.

«

When I was young
I studied styles: their use
and origin. Which age
was known for which
ornament: and was always drawn
to a lyric speech, a civil tone.
But never thought
I would have the need,
as I do now, for a darker one:

Spirit of irony,
my caustic author
of the past, of memory,—
and of its pain, which returns
hurts, stings—reproach me now,
remind me
that I was in those rooms,
with my child,
with my back turned to her,
searching—oh irony!—
for beautiful things.

Formal Feeling

A winged god
came to a woman at night.

Eros you know the story. You ordained it.

The one condition was she did not see him.

So it was dark when he visited her bed.
And it was good. She felt how good it was.
But she was curious. And lit a lamp.
And saw his nakedness. And he fled.

Into the dark. Into the here and now
and air and quiet of an Irish night
where I am writing at a darkening window
about a winged god and his lover,

watching the lines and stanzas and measures,
which were devised for these purposes,
disappearing as the shadows close
in around the page
under my hand.

How can I know a form unless I see it?
How can I see it now?
        ((

I propose
the light she raised over his sleeping body
angered heaven because it made clear
neither his maleness nor his birth, nor
his face dreaming, but

the place where the sinew of his wings
touched the heat of his skin
and flight was brought down—

To this. To us. To earth.

Eros look down.
See as a god sees
what a myth says: how a woman still
addresses the work of man in the dark of the night:

The power of a form. The plain
evidence that strength descended here once.
And mortal pain. And even sexual glory.

And see the difference.
This time—and this you did not ordain—
I am changing the story.

W h o s e ?

Beautiful land the patriot said
and rinsed it with his blood. And the sun rose.
And the river burned. The earth leaned
towards him: Shadows grew long. Ran red.

Beautiful land I whispered. But the roads
stayed put. Stars froze over the suburb.
Shadows iced up. Nothing moved.
Except my hand across the page. And these words.